1000 French words

compiled by John Williams BA (Hons)

Copyright © 1993 World International Publishing Limited.
All rights reserved.
Published in Great Britain by World International Publishing Limited,
an Egmont Company, Egmont House,
PO Box 111, Great Ducie Street,
Manchester M60 3BL.

Printed in Finland.
ISBN 0 7498 1435 7

A catalogue record for this book is available from the British Library.

contents

who are you? 5
people 6
the family 7
parts of the body 8
clothes 10
the home 12
rooms and furniture 13
in the bedroom 14
in the bathroom 15
eating and mealtimes 16
food and drink 17
vegetables 19
fruit 20
meat and fish 21
in the kitchen 22
in the garden 23
at school 24
school subjects 25
reading, writing and drawing 26
toys, games and pastimes 28
sport 30
music and singing 31
television 32
making things 33
containers 34
animals 35
birds, insects and small creatures 37
places 38
countries and continents 39
areas of water 41
buildings 41
shopping 42
people and their jobs 43
vehicles 44
moving, travelling and directions 45
things you do with your head 46
things you do with your hands 47
colours and shapes 48
describing people 49
describing things 51
numbers 53
other number words 55
time 56
telling the time 57
days of the week 58
seasons and festivals 58
months of the year 59
weather 60
things in the sky 61
where is it? where is it going? 62
questions and answers 63
useful little words 64

notes to readers

This book contains many of the most useful words you will need to know when you start learning French. However, on its own, it will not tell you how to speak or write correct French sentences. For that you will need a proper textbook, and probably a good teacher as well!

gender

There is one very important difference between French and English that you will need to know about right from the start. Every French **noun** (a word which means a thing, a person or an idea) belongs to one of two different types, or **genders**. These genders are called **masculine** and **feminine**. It is as if everything in the world was either 'he' (masculine) or 'she' (feminine). The idea of genders might seem rather strange when you are talking about objects. For instance, a moustache is feminine, whereas a woman's tights are masculine!

In this book we have tried to help you learn genders by showing each French noun, wherever we can, together with its word for 'a', 'an' or 'the', which change according to whether the noun is masculine or feminine.

With masculine nouns the word for 'a' or 'an' is **un** and with feminine nouns it is **une**. With most singular masculine nouns the word for 'the' is **le** and with feminine nouns it is **la**. So, whenever you learn a new noun you should also learn whether it takes **un** or **une**, **le** or **la**.

With a few nouns it is not possible to show the gender using these little words. In such cases we have shown the gender in brackets after the French word – **(m)** for masculine and **(f)** for feminine.

pronunciation

Under each French word we have shown its **pronunciation**, that is, the way it should be spoken. If you say these pronunciations as you would expect to say them in English, you will get quite close to the way the French words are actually spoken.

key to pronunciation

( )	Letters in brackets are pronounced only slightly or not at all.
a	Sounds like the 'a' sound in 'cat' or 'and'.
ah	Sounds like the 'a' sound in 'father' or 'calm'.
ay	Sounds like the 'ay' sound in 'say' or 'able'.
e	Sounds like the 'e' sound in 'let' or 'end'.
e(r)	Sounds like the 'e' sound in 'the'.
(n)	The sound *(n)* after a vowel means that the vowel is pronounced through the nose, as if there was a slight 'n' sound after it.
o	Sounds like the 'o' sound in 'hot' or 'odd'.
oh	Sounds like the 'o' sound in 'told' or 'rose'.
r	Sounds like the 'ch' sound in the Scottish word 'loch'.
s	Sounds like the 's' sound in 'say' or 'house'.
uh	Sounds like the 'ur' sound in 'fur', but the 'r' is silent.
y	Sounds like the 'y' sound in 'young'.
yoo	Sounds like the 'ew' sound in 'new'.
zh	Sounds like the 's' sound in 'treasure'.

accents

You will notice that some letters in French words have little marks, known as **accents**, above (or sometimes below) them. These are important parts of the spelling and often change the way a particular letter is pronounced.

The **acute accent** (´) is only ever found over the letter 'e'. The letter **é** is pronounced *ay*.

The **grave accent** (`) is found mainly over the letter 'e' and often shows that the *e* sound is pronounced slightly longer than usual. It is also found over the letters 'a' and 'u', but it does not change the pronunciation.

The **circumflex accent** (^) is found over the letters 'a', 'e', 'i', 'o' and 'u'. It shows that the vowel sound is pronounced slightly longer than usual.

The **cedilla** (ç) is only ever found under the letter 'c'. It is used to show the 'c' should be pronounced like an 's' and not a 'k'.

The **diaeresis** (¨) is uncommon. It is used to show that two vowels should be pronounced separately, and not together.

who are you?

address	une adresse	*yoon a-dres*
age	un âge	*uhn ahzh*
birthday	un anniversaire	*uhn a-nee-vair-sair*
boy	un garçon	*uh(n) gar-so(n)*
child	un enfant, une enfant	*uhn ah(n)-fah(n), yoon ah(n)-fah(n)*
girl	une fille	*yoon fee-y*
I	je	*zhe(r)*
I am	je suis	*zhe(r) swee*
my	mon, ma, mes	*mo(n), ma, may*
name	un nom	*uh(n) no(n)*
our	notre	*no-tr*
we	nous	*noo*
we are	nous sommes	*noo som*
you	vous	*voo*
you (to a friend)	tu	*tyoo*
your	votre	*vo-tr*
your (of a friend)	ton, ta, tes	*to(n), ta, tay*

people

baby	un bébé	*uh(n) bay-bay*
friend	un ami, une amie	*uhn a-mee. yoon a-mee*
gentleman	un monsieur	*uh(n) me(r)-syuh*
he	il	*eel*
lady	une dame	*yoon dam*
man	un homme	*uhn om*
Miss	Mademoiselle	*ma-de(r)-mwa-zel*
Mr	Monsieur	*me(r)-syuh*
Mrs	Madame	*ma-dam*
neighbour	un voisin, une voisine	*uh(n) vwa-za(n), yoon vwa-zeen*
people	les gens	*lay zhah(n)*
person	une personne	*yoon pair-son*
she	elle	*el*
somebody	quelqu'un	*kel-kuh(n)*
they	ils	*eel*
they (women and girls only)	elles	*el*
woman	une femme	*yoon fam*

the family

aunt	une tante	*yoon tah(n)t*
brother	un frère	*uh(n) frair*
cousin	un cousin, une cousine	*uh(n) koo-za(n), yoon koo-zeen*
daughter	une fille	*yoon fee-y*
family	une famille	*yoon fa-mee-y*
father	un père	*uh(n) pair*
grandfather	un grand-père	*uh(n) grah(n)-pair*
grandmother	une grand-mère	*yoon grah(n)-mair*
husband	un mari	*uh(n) ma-ree*
mother	une mère	*yoon mair*
nephew	un neveu	*uh(n) ne(r)-vuh*
niece	une nièce	*yoon nyes*
parents	les parents	*lay pa-rah(n)*
sister	une soeur	*yoon suhr*
son	un fils	*uh(n) fees*
uncle	un oncle	*uhn o(n)-kl*
wife	une femme	*yoon fam*

parts of the body

arm	un bras	*uh(n) bra*
back	un dos	*uh(n) doh*
body	un corps	*uh(n) kor*
brain	un cerveau	*uh(n) sair-voh*
chest	une poitrine	*yoon pwa-treen*
chin	un menton	*uh(n) mah(n)-to(n)*
ear	une oreille	*yoon o-ray-y*
elbow	un coude	*uh(n) kood*
eye	un oeil	*uhn uh-ee-y*
eyebrow	un sourcil	*uh(n) soor-see*
eyes	les yeux	*layz yuh*
face	un visage	*uh(n) vee-zazh*
finger	un doigt	*uh(n) dwa*
foot	un pied	*uh(n) pyay*
forehead	un front	*uh(n) fro(n)*
hair	les cheveux	*lay she(r)-vuh*
hand	une main	*yoon ma(n)*

head	une tête	*yoon tet*
heart	un coeur	*uh(n) kuhr*
knee	un genou	*uh(n) zhe(r)-noo*
leg	une jambe	*yoon zhah(n)b*
lip	une lèvre	*yoon le-vr*
mouth	une bouche	*yoon boosh*
nail	un ongle	*uhn o(n)-gl*
neck	un cou	*uh(n) koo*
nose	un nez	*uh(n) nay*
shoulder	une épaule	*yoon ay-pohl*
skin	la peau	*la poh*
stomach	un estomac	*uhn es-to-ma*
thumb	un pouce	*uh(n) poos*
toe	un doigt de pied	*uh(n) dwa de(r) pyay*
tongue	une langue	*yoon lah(n)g*
tooth	une dent	*yoon dah(n)*

clothes

belt	une ceinture	*yoon sa(n)-tyoor*
blouse	un corsage	*uh(n) kor-sazh*
boot	une botte	*yoon bot*
button	un bouton	*uh(n) boo-to(n)*
cap	une casquette	*yoon kas-ket*
a piece of clothing	un vêtement	*uh(n) vet-mah(n)*
coat	un manteau	*uh(n) mah(n)-toh*
dress	une robe	*yoon rob*
to dress, to get dressed	s'habiller	*sa-bee-yay*
glove	un gant	*uh(n) gah(n)*
hat	un chapeau	*uh(n) sha-poh*
jacket	une veste	*yoon vest*
knickers	une culotte	*yoon kyoo-lot*
pullover	un pull-over	*uh(n) poo-lo-vuhr*
to put on	mettre	*me-tr*
raincoat	un imperméable	*uhn a(n)-pair-may-abl*
scarf	une écharpe	*yoon ay-sharp*

English	French	Pronunciation
shirt	une chemise	yoon she(r)-meez
shoe	une chaussure	yoon shoh-syoor
shorts	un short	uh(n) short
skirt	une jupe	yoon zhyoop
sleeve	une manche	yoon mah(n)sh
sock	une chaussette	yoon shoh-set
sweatshirt	un sweat-shirt	uh(n) sweet-shuhrt
to take off	enlever	ah(n)-le(r)-vay
tie	une cravate	yoon kra-vat
tights	un collant	uh(n) ko-lah(n)
trousers	un pantalon	uh(n) pah(n)-ta-lo(n)
T-shirt	un tee-shirt	uh(n) tee-shuhrt
underpants	un slip	uh(n) sleep
to undress, to get undressed	se déshabiller	se(r) day-za-bee-yay
to wear	porter	por-tay

the home

carpet	un tapis	*uh(n) ta-pee*
ceiling	un plafond	*uh(n) pla-fo(n)*
chimney	une cheminée	*yoon she(r)-mee-nay*
curtain	un rideau	*uh(n) ree-doh*
door	une porte	*yoon port*
doorbell	une sonnette	*yoon so-net*
downstairs	en bas	*ah(n) ba*
flat	un appartement	*uhn a-par-te(r)-mah(n)*
floor	un plancher	*uh(n) plah(n)-shay*
house	une maison	*yoon me-zo(n)*
key	une clef	*yoon klay*
to live	habiter	*a-bee-tay*
roof	un toit	*uh(n) twa*
telephone	un téléphone	*uh(n) tay-lay-fon*
upstairs	en haut	*ah(n) oh*
wall	un mur	*uh(n) myoor*
window	une fenêtre	*yoon fe(r)-ne-tre*

rooms and furniture

a piece of furniture	un meuble	*uh(n) muh-bl*
armchair	un fauteuil	*uh(n) fo-tuh-ee-y*
attic	un grenier	*uh(n) gre-nyay*
bathroom	une salle de bain	*yoon sal de(r) ba(n)*
bedroom	une chambre	*yoon shah(n)-br*
chair	une chaise	*yoon shez*
cupboard	un placard	*uh(n) pla-kar*
dining room	une salle à manger	*yoon sal a mah(n)-zhay*
kitchen	une cuisine	*yoon kwee-zeen*
living room	une salle de séjour	*yoon sal de(r) say-zhoor*
room	une pièce	*yoon pyess*
settee, sofa	un canapé	*uh(n) ka-na-pay*
shelf	une étagère	*yoon ay-ta-zhair*
table	une table	*yoon ta-bl*
toilet	les toilettes (f)	*lay twa-let*
wardrobe	une garde-robe	*yoon gard-rob*

in the bedroom

bed	un lit	*uh(n) lee*
to go to bed	se coucher	*se(r) koo-shay*
blanket	une couverture	*yoon koo-vair-tyoor*
dream	un rêve	*uh(n) rev*
to dream	rêver	*re-vay*
dressing gown	une robe de chambre	*yoon rob de(r) shah(n)-br*
duvet	une couette	*yoon kwet*
to get up	se lever	*se(r) le(r)-vay*
lamp	une lampe	*yoon lah(n)p*
nightie	une chemise de nuit	*yoon she(r)-meez de(r) nwee*
pillow	un oreiller	*uhn o-ray-yay*
pyjamas	un pyjama	*uh(n) pee-zha-ma*
sheet	un drap	*uh(n) dra*
to sleep	dormir	*dor-meer*
to go to sleep	s'endormir	*sah(n)-dor-meer*
slipper	une pantoufle	*yoon pah(n)-too-fl*
to wake up	se réveiller	*se(r) ray-vay-yay*

in the bathroom

bath *(to have a bath)*	un bain *uh(n) ba(n)*
bath, bathtub	une baignoire *yoon ben-y-war*
comb	un peigne *uh(n) pen-y*
to comb your hair	se peigner *se(r) pe-nyay*
flannel	un gant de toilette *uh(n) gah(n) de(r) twa-let*
mirror	un miroir *uh(n) mee-rwar*
shampoo	le shampooing *le(r) shah(n)-pwa(n)*
shower	une douche *yoon doosh*
soap	le savon *le(r) sa-vo(n)*
sponge	une éponge *yoon ay-po(n)zh*
toilet	une cuvette de W.C. *yoon kyoo-vet de(r) vay-say*
toilet paper	le papier hygiénique *le(r) pa-pyay ee-zhyay-neek*
toothbrush	une brosse à dents *yoon bros a dah(n)*
toothpaste	le dentifrice *le(r) dah(n)-tee-frees*
towel	une serviette *yoon sair-vyet*
to wash	se laver *se(r) la-vay*
washbasin	un lavabo *uh(n) la-va-boh*

eating and mealtimes

bowl	un bol *uh(n) bol*
breakfast	le petit déjeuner *le(r) pe(r)-tee day-zhuh-nay*
cup	une tasse *yoon tas*
dinner (in the evening)	le dîner *le(r) dee-nay*
to drink	boire *bwar*
to eat	manger *mah(n)-zhay*
fork	une fourchette *yoon foor-shet*
glass	un verre *uh(n) vair*
I'm hungry	j'ai faim *zhay fa(n)*
knife	un couteau *uh(n) koo-toh*
lunch	le déjeuner *le(r) day-zhuh-nay*
meal	un repas *uh(n) re(r)-pa*
plate	une assiette *yoon a-syet*
saucer	une soucoupe *yoon soo-koop*
spoon	une cuiller *yoon kwee-yair*
supper (before bedtime)	une collation *yoon ko-la-syo(n)*
I'm thirsty	j'ai soif *zhay swaf*

food and drink

biscuit	un biscuit	*uh(n) bees-kwee*
bread	le pain	*le(r) pa(n)*
butter	le beurre	*le(r) buhr*
cake	un gâteau	*uh(n) ga-toh*
cheese	le fromage	*le(r) fro-mazh*
chips	les pommes frites (f)	*lay pom freet*
chocolate	le chocolat	*le(r) sho-ko-la*
coffee	le café	*le(r) ka-fay*
cream	la crème	*la krem*
crisps	les chips	*lay sheeps*
egg	un oeuf	*uhn uhf*
flour	la farine	*la fa-reen*
food	la nourriture	*la noo-ree-tyoor*
ice cream	une glace	*yoon glas*
jam	la confiture	*la ko(n)-fee-tyoor*
juice	le jus	*le(r) zhyoo*
lemonade	la limonade	*la lee-mo-nad*

margarine	la margarine	*la mar-ga-reen*
milk	le lait	*le(r) lay*
pepper	le poivre	*le(r) pwa-vr*
rice	le riz	*le(r) ree*
salad	une salade	*yoon sa-lad*
salt	le sel	*le(r) sel*
soup	la soupe	*la soop*
stew	un ragoût	*uh(n) ra-goo*
sugar	le sucre	*le(r) syoo-kr*
sweets	les bonbons (m)	*lay bo(n)-bo(n)*
tea	le thé	*le(r) tay*
toast	le pain grillé	*le(r) pa(n) gree-yay*
vinegar	le vinaigre	*le(r) vee-ne-gr*
water	l'eau (f)	*loh*
yoghourt	le yaourt	*le(r) ya-oort*

vegetables

bean	un haricot	*uh(n) a-ree-koh*
cabbage	un chou	*uh(n) shoo*
carrot	une carotte	*yoon ka-rot*
cauliflower	un chou-fleur	*uh(n) shoo-fluhr*
celery	le céleri	*le(r) sel-ree*
cucumber	un concombre	*uh(n) ko(n)-ko(n)-br*
leek	un poireau	*uh(n) pwa-roh*
lettuce	une salade	*yoon sa-lad*
mushroom	un champignon	*uh(n) shah(n)-pee-nyon*
onion	un oignon	*uhn o-nyo(n)*
peas	les petits pois (m)	*lay pe(r)-tee pwa*
potato	une pomme de terre	*yoon pom de(r) tair*
sprout	un chou de Bruxelles	*uh(n) shoo de(r) bryoo-sel*
sweetcorn	le maïs	*le(r) ma-ees*
tomato	une tomate	*yoon to-mat*
turnip	un navet	*uh(n) na-vay*
vegetable	un légume	*uh(n) lay-gyoom*

fruit

apple	une pomme	*yoon pom*
apricot	un abricot	*uhn a-bree-koh*
banana	une banane	*yoon ba-nan*
blackcurrant	un cassis	*uh(n) ka-sees*
cherry	une cerise	*yoon se(r)-reez*
fruit	un fruit	*uh(n) frwee*
grape	un raisin	*uh(n) re-za(n)*
grapefruit	un pamplemousse	*uh(n) pah(n)-ple(r)-moos*
lemon	un citron	*uh(n) see-tro(n)*
lime	un citron vert	*uh(n) see-tro(n) vair*
orange	une orange	*yoon o-rah(n)zh*
peach	une pêche	*yoon pesh*
pear	une poire	*yoon pwar*
pineapple	un ananas	*uhn a-na-nas*
plum	une prune	*yoon pryoon*
raspberry	une framboise	*yoon frah(n)-bwaz*
strawberry	une fraise	*yoon frez*

meat and fish

bacon	le lard	*le(r) lar*
beef	le boeuf	*le(r) buhf*
chicken	le poulet	*le(r) poo-lay*
chop	une côtelette	*yoon koht-let*
cod	la morue	*la mo-ryoo*
fish	le poisson	*le(r) pwa-so(n)*
fish finger	un bâtonnet de poisson	*uh(n) ba-to-nay de(r) pwa-so(n)*
ham	le jambon	*le(r) zhah(n)-bo(n)*
hamburger	un hamburger	*uh(n) ah(n)-boor-guhr*
lamb	l'agneau (m)	*la-nyoh*
meat	la viande	*la vyah(n)d*
pork	le porc	*le(r) por*
salmon	le saumon	*le(r) soh-mo(n)*
sausage	une saucisse	*yoon soh-sees*
steak	un bifteck	*uh(n) beef-tek*
tuna	le thon	*le(r) to(n)*
turkey	la dinde	*la da(n)d*

in the kitchen

apron	un tablier	*uh(n) ta-blee-yay*
to cook	faire la cuisine	*fair la kwee-zeen*
cooker	une cuisinière	*yoon kwee-zee-nyair*
dishcloth	une lavette	*yoon la-vet*
dishwasher	un lave-vaisselle	*uh(n) lav-ve-sel*
to fry	faire frire	*fair freer*
frying pan	une poêle	*yoon pwal*
grill	un gril	*uh(n) greel*
microwave	un four à micro-ondes	*uh(n) foor a mee-kroh-o(n)d*
oven	un four	*uh(n) foor*
pan	une casserole	*yoon kas-rol*
sieve	une passoire	*yoon pa-swar*
sink	un évier	*uhn ay-vyay*
tap	un robinet	*uh(n) ro-bee-nay*
tea towel	un torchon à vaisselle	*uh(n) tor-sho(n) a ve-sel*
to wash up	faire la vaisselle	*fair la ve-sel*
washing machine	une machine à laver	*yoon ma-sheen a la-vay*

in the garden

bush	un buisson	*uh(n) bwee-so(n)*
to dig	creuser	*kruh-zay*
flower	une fleur	*yoon fluhr*
garden	un jardin	*uh(n) zhar-da(n)*
gate	une porte	*yoon port*
grass	l'herbe (f)	*lairb*
lawn	une pelouse	*yoon pe(r)-looz*
lawnmower	une tondeuse à gazon	*yoon to(n)-duhz a ga-zo(n)*
leaf	une feuille	*yoon fuh-ee-y*
plant	une plante	*yoon plah(n)t*
soil	le sol	*le(r) sol*
spade	une bêche	*yoon besh*
tree	un arbre	*uhn ar-br*
to water	arroser	*a-roh-zay*
watering can	un arrosoir	*uhn a-roh-zwar*
weed	une mauvaise herbe	*yoon moh-vez airb*
wheelbarrow	une brouette	*yoon broo-et*

at school

blackboard	un tableau noir	*uh(n) ta-bloh nwar*
chalk	la craie	*la cray*
class	une classe	*yoon klas*
classroom	une salle de classe	*yoon sal de(r) klas*
desk	un pupitre	*uh(n) pyoo-pee-tr*
exam	un examen	*uhn eg-za-ma(n)*
head teacher	un directeur, une directrice	*uh(n) dee-rek-tuhr, yoon dee-rek-trees*
to learn	apprendre	*a-prah(n)-dr*
lesson	une leçon	*yoon le(r)-so(n)*
playground	une cour de récréation	*yoon koor de(r) ray-kray-a-syo(n)*
primary school	une école primaire	*yoon ay-col pree-mair*
pupil	un élève, une élève	*uhn ay-lev, yoon ay-lev*
school	une école	*yoon ay-col*
secondary school	un collège	*uh(n) ko-lezh*
to teach	enseigner	*ah(n)-se-nyay*
teacher	un professeur	*uh(n) pro-fe-suhr*
test	une interrogation	*yoon a(n)-te-ro-ga-syo(n)*

school subjects

arithmetic	l'arithmétique (f)	*la-reet-may-teek*
art	le dessin	*le(r) day-sa(n)*
chemistry	la chimie	*la shee-mee*
English	l'anglais (m)	*lah(n)-glay*
French	le français	*le(r) frah(n)-say*
games	le sport	*le(r) spor*
geography	la géographie	*la zhay-o-gra-fee*
German	l'allemand (m)	*lal-mah(n)*
history	l'histoire (f)	*lees-twar*
mathematics	les mathématiques (f)	*lay ma-tay-ma-teek*
music	la musique	*la myoo-zeek*
nature study	l'histoire naturelle (f)	*lees-twar na-tyoo-rel*
physical education	l'éducation physique (f)	*lay-dyoo-ka-syo(n) fee-zeek*
physics	la physique	*la fee-zeek*
religious education	l'instruction religieuse (f)	*la(n)-stryook-syo(n) re(r)-lee-zhyuhz*
science	les sciences (f)	*lay see-ah(n)s*
subject	une matière	*yoon ma-tyair*

reading, writing and drawing

alphabet	l'alphabet (m)	*lal-fa-bay*
book	un livre	*uh(n) lee-vr*
capital letter	une majuscule	*yoon ma-zhyoo-skyool*
comic	un magazine de bandes dessinées	*uh(n) ma-ga-zeen de(r) bah(n)d day-see-nay*
comma	une virgule	*yoon veer-gyool*
to copy	copier	*ko-pyay*
crayon	un crayon de couleur	*uh(n) kray-yo(n) de(r) koo-luhr*
to draw	dessiner	*day-see-nay*
envelope	une enveloppe	*yoon ah(n)-vlop*
exercise book	un cahier	*uh(n) ka-yay*
full stop	un point	*uh(n) pwa(n)*
letter *(that you send)*	une lettre	*yoon le-tr*
line	une ligne	*yoon leen-y*
magazine	un magazine	*uh(n) ma-ga-zeen*
newspaper	un journal	*uh(n) zhoor-nal*
page	une page	*yoon pazh*

to paint	peindre	*pa(n)-dr*
paper	le papier	*le(r) pa-pyay*
pen	un stylo	*uh(n) stee-lo*
pencil	un crayon	*uh(n) cray-yo(n)*
pencil sharpener	un taille-crayon	*uh(n) ta-y-cray-yo(n)*
picture	une image	*yoon ee-mazh*
poem	un poème	*uh(n) poh-em*
question mark	un point d'interrogation	*uh(n) pwa(n) da(n)-tay-ro-ga-syo(n)*
to read	lire	*leer*
rubber	une gomme	*yoon gom*
ruler	une règle	*yoon re-gl*
sentence	une phrase	*yoon fraz*
story	une histoire	*yoon ee-stwar*
to spell	épeler	*ay-play*
spelling	l'orthographe (f)	*lor-to-graf*
word	un mot	*uh(n) moh*
to write	écrire	*ay-kreer*

toys, games and pastimes

board game	un jeu de société	*uh(n) zhuh de(r) so-syay-tay*
camera	un appareil-photo	*uhn a-pa-ray-y-foh-toh*
cassette, tape	une cassette	*yoon ka-set*
chess	les échecs (m)	*layz ay-shek*
to collect	collectionner	*ko-lek-syo-nay*
compact disc	un disque compact	*uh(n) deesk ko(n)-pakt*
computer	un ordinateur	*uhn or-dee-na-tuhr*
to dance	danser	*dah(n)-say*
dice	un dé	*uh(n) day*
doll	une poupée	*yoon poo-pay*
doll's house	une maison de poupée	*yoon me-zo(n) de(r) poo-pay*
fishing	la pêche	*la pesh*
game	un jeu	*uh(n) zhuh*
hide-and-seek	le cache-cache	*le(r) kash-kash*
hobby	un passe-temps	*uh(n) pas-tah(n)*
hopscotch	la marelle	*la ma-rel*

jigsaw	un puzzle	*uh(n) puh-zl*
leap-frog	le saute-mouton	*le(r) soht-moo-to(n)*
model	un modèle	*uh(n) mo-del*
photo	une photo	*yoon foh-toh*
to play	jouer	*zhway*
playing card	une carte à jouer	*yoon kart a zhway*
radio	une radio	*yoon ra-dyoh*
record	un disque	*uh(n) deesk*
roller skate	un patin à roulettes	*uh(n) pa-ta(n) a roo-let*
skateboard	une planche à roulettes	*yoon plah(n)sh a roo-let*
stamp	un timbre	*uh(n) ta(n)-br*
stereo	une chaîne stéréo	*yoon shen stay-ray-oh*
teddy bear	un ours en peluche	*uhn oors ah(n) pe(r)-lyoosh*
toy	un jouet	*uh(n) zhway*
toy soldier	un petit soldat	*uh(n) pe(r)-tee sol-da*
train set	un train électrique	*uh(n) tra(n) ay-lek-treek*

sport

ball	une balle	*yoon bal*
cricket	le cricket	*le(r) kree-ket*
football (sport)	le football	*le foot-bohl*
football (ball)	un ballon	*uh(n) ba-lo(n)*
football boot	une chaussure de football	*yoon shoh-syoor de(r) foot-bohl*
football match	un match de football	*uh(n) matsh de(r) foot-bohl*
to lose	perdre	*pair-dr*
snooker	un jeu de billard	*uh(n) zhuh de(r) bee-yar*
sport	un sport	*uh(n) spor*
to swim	nager	*na-zhay*
swimming	la natation	*la na-ta-syo(n)*
swimming costume	un maillot de bain	*uh(n) ma-yoh de(r) ba(n)*
swimming pool	une piscine	*yoon pee-seen*
table tennis	le tennis de table	*le(r) te-nees de(r) ta-bl*
tennis	le tennis	*le(r) te-nees*
tracksuit	un survêtement	*uh(n) syoor-vet-mah(n)*
to win	gagner	*ga-nyay*

music and singing

choir	un chœur	*uh(n) kuhr*
drum	un tambour	*uh(n) tah(n)-boor*
guitar	une guitare	*yoon gee-tar*
hymn	une hymne	*yoon eemn*
instrument	un instrument	*uhn a(n)-stryoo-mah(n)*
orchestra	un orchestre	*uhn or-kes-tr*
organ	un orgue	*uhn org*
piano	le piano	*le(r) pya-noh*
pop music	la musique pop	*la myoo-zeek pop*
recorder	une flûte à bec	*yoon flyoot a bek*
to sing	chanter	*shah(n)-tay*
singer	un chanteur, une chanteuse	*uh(n) shah(n)-tuhr, yoon shah(n)-tuhz*
song	une chanson	*yoon shah(n)-so(n)*
trumpet	une trompette	*yoon tro(n)-pet*
tune	un air	*uhn air*
violin	un violon	*uh(n) vyo-lo(n)*
voice	une voix	*yoon vwa*

television

advert	une publicité	*yoon pyoo-blee-see-tay*
aerial	une antenne	*yoon ah(n)-ten*
cartoon	un dessin animé	*uh(n) day-sa(n) a-nee-may*
channel	une chaîne	*yoon shen*
comedy	une comédie	*yoon ko-may-dee*
film	un film	*uh(n) feelm*
news	les informations (f)	*lay za(n)-for-ma-syo(n)*
programme	une émission	*yoon ay-mee-syo(n)*
quiz	un jeu-concours	*uh(n) zhuh-ko(n)-koor*
remote control	une télécommande	*yoon tay-lay-ko-mah(n)d*
screen	un écran	*uhn ay-krah(n)*
television	une télévision	*yoon tay-lay-vee-zyo(n)*
to turn off	éteindre	*ay-ta(n)-dr*
to turn on	allumer	*a-lyoo-may*
video recorder	un magnétoscope	*uh(n) ma-nyay-to-skop*
video tape	une vidéocassette	*yoon vee-day-oh-ka-set*
to watch	regarder	*re(r)-gar-day*

32

making things

to build	bâtir	*ba-teer*
cardboard	le carton	*le(r) kar-to(n)*
glass	le verre	*le(r) vair*
glue	la colle	*la kol*
hammer	un marteau	*uh(n) mar-toh*
to knit	tricoter	*tree-ko-tay*
metal	un métal	*uh(n) may-tal*
nail	un clou	*uh(n) kloo*
needle	une aiguille	*yoon ay-gwee-y*
plastic	le plastique	*le(r) pla-steek*
saw	une scie	*yoon see*
scissors	les ciseaux (m)	*lay see-zoh*
to sew	coudre	*koo-dr*
to stick	coller	*ko-lay*
string	la ficelle	*la fee-sel*
wood	le bois	*le(r) bwa*
wool	la laine	*la len*

containers

bag	un sac	*uh(n) sak*
bottle	une bouteille	*yoon boo-tay-y*
box	une boîte	*yoon bwat*
bucket	un seau	*uh(n) soh*
cage	une cage	*yoon kazh*
drawer	un tiroir	*uh(n) tee-rwar*
handbag	un sac à main	*uh(n) sak a ma(n)*
jar	un pot à confitures	*uh(n) poh a ko(n)-fee-tyoor*
jug	un pot	*uh(n) poh*
kettle	une bouilloire	*yoon boo-y-war*
packet	un paquet	*uh(n) pa-kay*
pocket	une poche	*yoon posh*
purse	un porte-monnaie	*uh(n) port-mo-nay*
suitcase	une valise	*yoon va-leez*
teapot	une théière	*yoon tay-yair*
tin	une boîte en métal	*yoon bwat ah(n) may-tal*
wallet	un portefeuille	*uh(n) port-fuh-ee-y*

animals

animal	un animal	*uhn a-nee-mal*
bear	un ours	*uhn oors*
bull	un taureau	*uh(n) toh-roh*
camel	un chameau	*uh(n) sha-moh*
cat	un chat	*uh(n) sha*
cow	une vache	*yoon vash*
dog	un chien	*uh(n) shya(n)*
donkey	un âne	*uhn an*
elephant	un éléphant	*uhn ay-lay-fah(n)*
fish	un poisson	*uh(n) pwa-so(n)*
fox	un renard	*uh(n) re(r)-nar*
frog	une grenouille	*yoon gre(r)-noo-y*
giraffe	une girafe	*yoon zhee-raf*
goldfish	un poisson rouge	*uh(n) pwa-so(n) roozh*
gorilla	une gorille	*yoon go-ree-y*
guinea pig	un cochon d'Inde	*uh(n) ko-sho(n) da(n)d*
hamster	un hamster	*uh(n) am-stair*

horse	un cheval	*uh(n) she(r)-val*
kitten	un petit chat	*uh(n) pe(r)-tee sha*
lamb	un agneau	*uhn a-nyoh*
lion	un lion	*uh(n) lyo(n)*
monkey	un singe	*uh(n) sa(n)zh*
mouse	une souris	*yoon soo-ree*
pig	un cochon	*uh(n) ko-sho(n)*
puppy	un jeune chien	*uh(n) zhuhn shya(n)*
rabbit	un lapin	*uh(n) la-pa(n)*
rat	un rat	*uh(n) ra*
rhinoceros	un rhinocéros	*uh(n) ree-no-say-ros*
sheep	un mouton	*uh(n) moo-to(n)*
snake	un serpent	*uh(n) sair-pah(n)*
tiger	un tigre	*uh(n) tee-gr*
tortoise	une tortue	*yoon tor-tyoo*
turtle	une tortue de mer	*yoon tor-tyoo de mair*
zebra	un zèbre	*uh(n) ze-br*

birds, insects and small creatures

ant	une fourmi	*yoon foor-mee*
bee	une abeille	*yoon a-bay-y*
bird	un oiseau	*uhn wa-zoh*
butterfly	un papillon	*uh(n) pa-pee-yo(n)*
duck	un canard	*uh(n) ka-nar*
eagle	un aigle	*uhn e-gl*
fly	une mouche	*yoon moosh*
hen	une poule	*yoon pool*
moth	un papillon de nuit	*uh(n) pa-pee-yo(n) de(r) nwee*
parrot	un perroquet	*uh(n) pe-ro-kay*
pigeon	un pigeon	*un pi-zho(n)*
snail	un escargot	*uhn es-car-goh*
sparrow	un moineau	*uh(n) mwa-noh*
spider	une araignée	*yoon a-ray-nyay*
swan	un cygne	*uh(n) seen-y*
wasp	une guêpe	*yoon gep*

places

airport	un aéroport	*uhn a-ay-ro-por*
beach	une plage	*yoon plazh*
city	une grande ville	*yoon grah(n)d veel*
continent	un continent	*uh(n) ko(n)-tee-nah(n)*
country	un pays	*uh(n) pay-ee*
countryside	la campagne	*la kah(n)-pan-y*
desert	un désert	*uh(n) day-zair*
farm	une ferme	*yoon fairm*
field	un champ	*uh(n) shah(n)*
mountain	une montagne	*yoon mo(n)-tan-y*
park	un parc	*uh(n) park*
place	un endroit	*uhn ah(n)-drwa*
road	une route	*yoon root*
station	une gare	*yoon gar*
street	une rue	*yoon ryoo*
town	une ville	*yoon veel*
village	un village	*uh(n) vee-lazh*

countries and continents

Africa	l'Afrique (f)	*la-freek*
America	l'Amérique (f)	*la-may-reek*
Argentina	l'Argentine (f)	*lar-zhah(n)-teen*
Asia	l'Asie (f)	*la-zee*
Australia	l'Australie (f)	*lo-stra-lee*
Austria	l'Autriche (f)	*loh-treesh*
Belgium	la Belgique	*la bel-zheek*
Brazil	le Brésil	*le(r) bray-zeel*
Britain	le Grande Bretagne	*la grah(n)d bre(r)-tan-y*
Canada	le Canada	*le(r) ka-na-da*
China	la Chine	*la sheen*
England	l'Angleterre (f)	*lah(n)-gle(r)-tair*
Europe	l'Europe (f)	*luh-rop*
France	la France	*la frah(n)s*
Germany	l'Allemagne (f)	*lal-man-y*
Greece	la Grèce	*la gres*
Holland	la Hollande	*la o-lah(n)d*

India	l'Inde (f)	
	la(n)d	
Ireland	l'Irlande (f)	
	leer-lah(n)d	
Italy	l'Italie (f)	
	lee-ta-lee	
Japan	le Japon	
	le(r) zha-po(n)	
New Zealand	la Nouvelle-Zélande	
	la noo-vel-zay-lah(n)d	
Pakistan	le Pakistan	
	le(r) pa-kee-stah(n)	
Portugal	le Portugal	
	le(r) por-tyoo-gal	
Russia	la Russie	
	la ryoo-see	
Scotland	l'Écosse (f)	
	lay-kos	
South Africa	l'Afrique du Sud (f)	
	la-freek dyoo syood	
Spain	l'Espagne (f)	
	les-pan-y	
Switzerland	la Suisse	
	la swees	
U.S.A.	les États-Unis (m)	
	layz ay-ta-zyoo-nee	
Wales	le pays de Galles	
	le(r) pay-ee de(r) gal	
West Indies	les Antilles (f)	
	layz ah(n)-tee-y	

areas of water

canal	un canal	*uh(n) ka-nal*
lake	un lac	*uh(n) lak*
ocean	un océan	*uhn oh-say-ah(n)*
pond	un étang	*uhn ay-tah(n)*
river	une rivière	*yoon ree-vyair*
sea	une mer	*yoon mair*
stream	un ruisseau	*uh(n) rwee-soh*

buildings

block of flats	un immeuble	*uhn ee-muh-bl*
building	un bâtiment	*uh(n) ba-tee-mah(n)*
church	une église	*yoon ay-gleez*
factory	une usine	*yoon yoo-zeen*
hospital	un hôpital	*uhn o-pee-tal*
hotel	un hôtel	*uhn oh-tel*
museum	un musée	*uh(n) myoo-zay*
office	un bureau	*uh(n) byoo-roh*

shopping

bank	une banque	*yoon bah(n)k*
to buy	acheter	*ash-tay*
change (money)	la monnaie	*la mo-nay*
chemist's	une pharmacie	*yoon far-ma-see*
department store	un grand magasin	*uh(n) grah(n) ma-ga-za(n)*
greengrocer's	une fruiterie	*yoon frwee-tree*
grocer's	une épicerie	*yoon ay-pee-sree*
market	un marché	*uh(n) mar-shay*
money	l'argent (m)	*lar-zhah(n)*
newsagent's	un marchand de journaux	*uh(n) mar-shah(n) de(r) zhoor-noh*
pet shop	une boutique d'animaux	*yoon boo-teek da-nee-moh*
post office	un bureau de poste	*uh(n) byoo-roh de(r) post*
to sell	vendre	*vah(n)-dr*
shop	un magasin	*uh(n) ma-ga-za(n)*
to spend	dépenser	*day-pah(n)-say*
supermarket	un supermarché	*uh(n) syoo-pair-mar-shay*
toy shop	un magasin de jouets	*uh(n) ma-ga-za(n) de zhway*

people and their jobs

bus conductor	un receveur d'autobus	*uh(n) re(r)-se(r)-vuhr doh-toh-byoos*
doctor	un docteur	*uh(n) dok-tuhr*
driver	un conducteur, une conductrice	*uh(n) ko(n)-dyook-tuhr, yoon ko(n)-dyook-trees*
farmer	un agriculteur	*uhn a-gree-kyool-tuhr*
fireman	un pompier	*uh(n) po(n)-pyay*
job	un emploi	*uhn ah(n)-plwa*
king	un roi	*uh(n) rwa*
nurse	une infirmière	*yoon a(n)-feer-myair*
policeman	un agent de police	*uhn a-zhah(n) de(r) po-lees*
policewoman	une femme-agent	*yoon fam-a-zhah(n)*
postman	un facteur	*uh(n) fak-tuhr*
queen	une reine	*yoon ren*
shopkeeper	un commerçant, une commerçante	*uh(n) ko-mair-sah(n), yoon ko-mair-sah(n)t*
soldier	un soldat	*uh(n) sol-da*
vet	un vétérinaire, une vétérinaire	*uh(n) vay-tay-ree-nair, yoon vay-tay-ree-nair*
work	le travail	*le(r) tra-va-y*
to work	travailler	*tra-va-yay*

43

vehicles

aeroplane	un avion	*uhn a-vyo(n)*
bicycle	une bicyclette	*yoon bee-see-klet*
boat	un bateau	*uh(n) ba-toh*
bus	un autobus	*uhn oh-toh-byoos*
car	une voiture	*yoon vwa-tyoor*
helicopter	un hélicoptère	*uhn ay-lee-kop-tair*
lorry	un camion	*uh(n) ka-myo(n)*
motorbike	une moto	*yoon moh-toh*
ship	un navire	*uh(n) na-veer*
spaceship	un vaisseau spatial	*uh(n) ve-soh spa-syal*
tank	un char	*uh(n) shar*
taxi	un taxi	*uh(n) tak-see*
tractor	un tracteur	*uh(n) trak-tuhr*
train	un train	*uh(n) tra(n)*
van	une camionnette	*yoon ka-myo-net*
vehicle	un véhicule	*uh(n) vay-ee-kyool*
wheel	une roue	*yoon roo*

moving, travelling and directions

| to arrive | arriver |
| | *a-ree-vay* |

| to climb | grimper |
| | *gra(n)-pay* |

| to drive | conduire |
| | *ko(n)-dweer* |

| east | l'est (m) |
| | *lest* |

| to fly | voler |
| | *vo-lay* |

| holiday | les vacances (f) |
| | *lay va-kah(n)s* |

| journey | un voyage |
| | *uh(n) vwa-yazh* |

| to jump | sauter |
| | *soh-tay* |

| to leave | partir |
| | *par-teer* |

| left | la gauche |
| | *la gohsh* |

| north | le nord |
| | *le(r) nor* |

| right | la droite |
| | *la drwat* |

| to run | courir |
| | *koo-reer* |

| south | le sud |
| | *le(r) syood* |

| to walk | marcher |
| | *mar-shay* |

| west | l'ouest (m) |
| | *lwest* |

45

things you do with your head

to cough	tousser	*too-say*
to cry	pleurer	*pluh-ray*
to forget	oublier	*oo-blee-yay*
to hear	entendre	*ah(n)-tah(n)-dr*
to laugh	rire	*reer*
to listen	écouter	*ay-koo-tay*
to look, to look at	regarder	*re(r)-gar-day*
to say, to tell	dire	*deer*
to remember	se rappeler	*se(r) ra-play*
to see	voir	*vwar*
to shout	crier	*kree-yay*
to smell	sentir	*sah(n)-teer*
to smile	sourire	*soo-reer*
to sneeze	éternuer	*ay-tair-nway*
to speak	parler	*par-lay*
to taste	goûter	*goo-tay*

things you do with your hands

to bring	apporter	*a-por-tay*
to carry	porter	*por-tay*
to catch	attraper	*a-tra-pay*
to close	fermer	*fair-may*
to lift	soulever	*sool-vay*
to give	donner	*do-nay*
to hold	tenir	*te(r)-neer*
to open	ouvrir	*oo-vreer*
to pick up	ramasser	*ra-ma-say*
to pull	tirer	*tee-ray*
to push	pousser	*poo-say*
to put	mettre	*me-tr*
to scratch	gratter	*gra-tay*
to take	prendre	*prah(n)-dr*
to throw	lancer	*lah(n)-say*
to touch	toucher	*too-shay*

colours and shapes

black	noir	*nwar*
blue	bleu	*bluh*
brown	brun	*bruh(n)*
circle	un cercle	*uh(n) sair-kl*
colour	une couleur	*yoon koo-luhr*
green	vert	*vair*
grey	gris	*gree*
orange	orange	*o-rah(n) zh*
pink	rose	*rohz*
purple	violet, violette	*vyo-lay, vyo-let*
rectangle	un rectangle	*uh(n) rek-tah(n)-gl*
red	rouge	*roozh*
shape	une forme	*yoon form*
square	un carré	*uh(n) ka-ray*
triangle	un triangle	*uh(n) tree-yah(n)-gl*
white	blanc, blanche	*blah(n), blah(n)sh*
yellow	jaune	*zhohn*

describing people

angry	fâché	*fa-shay*
beautiful	belle	*bel*
brave	courageux, courageuse	*koo-ra-zhuh, koo-ra-zhuhz*
clever	intelligent	*a(n)-tay-lee-zhah(n)*
dishonest	malhonnête	*ma-lo-net*
fat	gras, grasse	*gra, gras*
friendly	sympathique	*sa(n)-pa-teek*
handsome	beau	*boh*
happy	heureux, heureuse	*uh-ruh, uh-ruhz*
healthy	sain	*sa(n)*
honest	honnête	*o-net*
kind	gentil, gentille	*zhah(n)-tee, zhah(n)-tee-y*
naughty	méchant	*may-shah(n)*
old	vieux, vieille	*vyuh, vyay-y*
polite	poli	*po-lee*
poor	pauvre	*poh-vr*
pretty	joli	*zho-lee*

rich	riche	*reesh*
rude	impoli	*a(n)-po-lee*
sad	triste	*treest*
short	petit	*pe(r)-tee*
sick	malade	*ma-lad*
slim	mince	*ma(n)s*
strong	fort	*for*
stupid	stupide	*styoo-peed*
tall	grand	*grah(n)*
tired	fatigué	*fa-tee-gay*
ugly	laid	*lay*
unfriendly	peu sympathique	*puh sa(n)-pa-teek*
weak	faible	*fe-bl*
young	jeune	*zhuhn*

describing things

bad	mauvais	*moh-vay*
big, large	grand	*grah(n)*
bright	clair	*klair*
cheap	bon marché	*bo(n) mar-shay*
dark	obscur	*ops-kyoor*
deep	profond	*pro-fo(n)*
difficult	difficile	*dee-fee-seel*
dry	sec, sèche	*sek, sesh*
easy	facile	*fa-seel*
expensive	cher	*shair*
false	faux, fausse	*foh, fohs*
flat	plat	*pla*
good	bon, bonne	*bo(n), bon*
hard	dur	*dyoor*
heavy	lourd	*dyoor*
high	haut	*oh*
interesting	intéressant	*a(n)-tay-re-sah(n)*

light (in weight)	léger, légère *lay-zhay, lay-zhair*
long	long, longue *lo(n), lo(n)g*
low	bas, basse *ba, bas*
narrow	étroit *ay-trwa*
new	nouveau, nouvelle *noo-voh, noo-vel*
old	vieux, vieille *vyuh, vyay-y*
quick	rapide *ra-peed*
round	rond *ro(n)*
short	court *koor*
slow	lent *lah(n)*
small, little	petit *pe(r)-tee*
soft	mou, molle *moo, mol*
thick	épais, épaisse *ay-pay, ay-pes*
thin	mince *ma(n)s*
true	vrai *vray*
wet	mouillé *moo-yay*
wide	large *larzh*

numbers

1	un, une	*uh(n), yoon*
2	deux	*duh*
3	trois	*trwa*
4	quatre	*ka-tr*
5	cinq	*sa(n)k*
6	six	*sees*
7	sept	*set*
8	huit	*weet*
9	neuf	*nuhf*
10	dix	*dees*
11	onze	*o(n)z*
12	douze	*dooz*
13	treize	*trez*
14	quatorze	*ka-torz*
15	quinze	*ka(n)z*
16	seize	*sez*
17	dix-sept	*dee-set*

18	dix-huit	*deez-weet*
19	dix-neuf	*deez-nuhf*
20	vingt	*va(n)*
21	vingt-et-un	*va(n)-tay-uh(n)*
22	vingt-deux	*va(n)t-duh*
23	vingt-trois	*va(n)t-trwa*
30	trente	*trah(n)t*
31	trente-et-un	*trah(n)t ay uh(n)*
32	trente-deux	*trah(n)t-duh*
40	quarante	*ka-rah(n)t*
50	cinquante	*sa(n)-kah(n)t*
60	soixante	*swa-sah(n)t*
70	soixante-dix	*swa-sah(n)t-dees*
80	quatre-vingts	*ka-tre(r)-va(n)*
90	quatre-vingt-dix	*ka-tre(r)-va(n)-dees*
100	cent	*sah(n)*
1,000	mille	*meel*

other number words

first	premier, première *pre(r)-myay, pre(r)-myair*
second	deuxième *duh-zyem*
third	troisième *trwa-zyem*
fourth	quatrième *ka-tree-yem*
fifth	cinquième *sa(n)-kyem*
once	une fois *yoon fwa*
twice	deux fois *duh fwa*
half	un demi *uh(n) de(r)-mee*
quarter	un quart *uh(n) kar*
to add	ajouter *a-zhoo-tay*
to count	compter *ko(n)-tay*
to divide	diviser *dee-vee-zay*
to multiply	multiplier *myool-tee-plee-yay*
number (1, 2, 3, etc.)	un numéro *uh(n) nyoo-may-roh*
number (a number of things)	un nombre *uh(n) no(n)-br*
to subtract	soustraire *soos-trair*
sum	un calcul *uh (n) Kal-Kyool*

time

afternoon	un après-midi *uhn a-pre-mee-dee*
calendar	un calendrier *uh(n) ka-lah(n)-dree-yay*
century	un siècle *uh(n) sye-kl*
clock	une pendule *yoon pah(n)-dyool*
date	une date *yoon dat*
dawn	l'aube (f) *lohb*
day	un jour *uh(n) zhoor*
early	tôt *toh*
evening	un soir *uh(n) swar*
hour	une heure *yoon uhr*
late	tard *tar*
leap year	une année bissextile *yoon a-nay bee-seks-teel*
midday	midi (m) *mee-dee*
midnight	minuit (m) *mee-nwee*
minute	une minute *yoon mee-nyoot*
month	un mois *uh(n) mwa*
morning	un matin *uh(n) ma-ta(n)*

night	une nuit	*yoon nwee*
second	une seconde	*yoon se(r)-go(n)d*
soon	bientôt	*bya(n)-toh*
time	le temps	*le(r) tah(n)*
time (on the clock)	l'heure (f)	*luhr*
today	aujourd'hui	*oh-zhoor-dwee*
tomorrow	demain	*de(r)-ma(n)*
week	une semaine	*yoon se(r)-men*
weekend	un week-end	*uh(n) wee-kend*
year	un an, une année	*uhn ah(n), yoon a-nay*
yesterday	hier	*yair*

telling the time

nine o'clock	neuf heures	*nuh vuhr*
half past nine	neuf heures et demie	*nuh vuhr ay de(r)-mee*
quarter past nine	neuf heures et quart	*nuh vuhr ay kar*
quarter to nine	neuf heures moins le quart	*nuh vuhr mwa(n) le(r) kar*

the days of the week

Monday	lundi (m)	*luh(n)-dee*
Tuesday	mardi (m)	*mar-dee*
Wednesday	mercredi (m)	*mair-cre(r)-dee*
Thursday	jeudi (m)	*zhuh-dee*
Friday	vendredi (m)	*vah(n)-dre(r)-dee*
Saturday	samedi (m)	*sam-dee*
Sunday	dimanche (m)	*dee-mah(n)sh*

seasons and festivals

autumn	l'automne (m)	*loh-ton*
Christmas	Noël (m or f)	*noh-el*
Easter	Pâques (m)	*pak*
New Year's Day	le jour de l'an	*le(r) zhoor de(r) lah(n)*
season	une saison	*yoon se-zo(n)*
spring	le printemps	*le(r) pra(n)-tah(n)*
summer	l'été (m)	*lay-tay*
winter	l'hiver (m)	*lee-vair*

months of the year

January	janvier (m)	*zhah(n)-vyay*
February	février (m)	*fay-vree-yay*
March	mars (m)	*mars*
April	avril (m)	*a-vreel*
May	mai (m)	*may*
June	juin (m)	*zhwa(n)*
July	juillet (m)	*zhwee-yay*
August	août (m)	*oot*
September	septembre (m)	*sep-tah(n)-br*
October	octobre (m)	*ok-to-br*
November	novembre (m)	*no-vah(n)-br*
December	décembre (m)	*day-sah(n)-br*

weather

cloud	un nuage	*uh(n) nyoo-azh*
cloudy	nuageux, nuageuse	*nyoo-a-zhuh. nyoo-a-zhuhz*
cold	froid	*frwa*
fog	le brouillard	*le(r) broo-yar*
it's foggy	il fait du brouillard	*eel fay dyoo broo-yar*
to freeze	geler	*zhe(r)-lay*
hot	chaud	*shoh*
ice	la glace	*la glas*
lightning	un éclair	*uhn ay-klair*
mist	la brume	*la bryoom*
rain	la pluie	*la plwee*
to rain	pleuvoir	*pluh-vwar*
rainy	pluvieux, pluvieuse	*plyoo-vyuh, plyoo-vyuhz*
shower	une averse	*yoon a-vairs*
snow	la neige	*la nezh*
to snow	neiger	*ne-zhay*
storm	un orage	*uhn o-razh*

sunshine	**le soleil** *le(r) so-lay-y*
thunder	**le tonnerre** *le(r) to-nair*
umbrella	**un parapluie** *uh(n) pa-ra-plwee*
warm	**chaud** *shoh*
weather	**le temps** *le(r) tah(n)*
wind	**le vent** *le(r) vah(n)*
it's windy	**il fait du vent** *eel fay dyoo vah(n)*

things in the sky

moon	**la lune** *la lyoon*
planet	**une planète** *yoon pla-net*
sky	**le ciel** *le(r) syel*
star	**une étoile** *yoon ay-twal*
sun	**le soreil** *le(r) so-lay-y*

61

where is it? where is it going?

above	au-dessus de	*oh-de(r)-syoo de(r)*
along	le long de	*le(r) lo(n) de(r)*
at	à	*a*
behind	derrière	*de-ryair*
between	entre	*ah(n)-tr*
in	dans	*dah(n)*
in front of	devant	*de(r)-vah(n)*
into	dans	*dah(n)*
next to	à côté de	*a koh-tay de(r)*
on	sur	*syoor*
out of	hors de	*or de(r)*
outside	dehors	*de(r)-or*
through	à travers	*a tra-vair*
to	à	*a*
towards	vers	*vair*
under	sous	*soo*

questions and answers

how?	comment? *ko-mah(n)*
how many? how much?	combien? *ko(n)-bya(n)*
what?	qu'est-ce que? *kes-ke(r)*
where?	où? *oo*
when?	quand? *kah(n)*
which?	quel? quelle? *kel*
who?	qui? *kee*
whose?	à qui? *a kee*
why?	pourquoi? *poor-kwa*
answer	une réponse *yoon ray-po(n)s*
to answer	répondre *ray-po(n)-dr*
to ask	demander *de(r)-mah(n)-day*
to ask a question	poser une question *poh-zay yoon kes-tyo(n)*
if, whether	si *see*
to guess	deviner *de(r)-vee-nay*
to know	savoir *sa-vwar*
question	une question *yoon kes-tyo(n)*

useful little words

also	aussi	*oh-see*
and	et	*ay*
because	parce que	*pars ke(r)*
but	mais	*may*
for	pour	*poor*
goodbye	au revoir	*oh re(r)-vwar*
hello	bonjour	*bo(n)-zhoor*
a lot	beaucoup	*boh-koo*
no	non	*no(n)*
not	ne...pas	*ne(r)...pa*
of	de	*de(r)*
please	s'il vous plaît	*see(l) voo play*
thank you	merci	*mair-see*
very	très	*tray*
with	avec	*a-vek*
without	sans	*sah(n)*
yes	oui	*wee*